Praise for *H*

"Scott Starbuck's *Hawk on Wire: E*
From his considerable experience with or the wild world ...... g
projection of our future, thanks mainly to our own ravishing of it. But
this grim vision is usually accompanied by the beckoning of a spirit world
beyond impending disaster. So it is in these mainly aphoristic poems, some
of which feature ghosts of already passed-away luminaries speaking of
climate change, such as Galileo and Mother Teresa. The ghost of Charles
Bukowski admonishes us by saying 'we must find / some way // to make
joy / no matter what.' This is a wonderful, bracing, and searching book,
lovingly and expertly written."
—John Keeble, author of *Yellowfish, Broken Ground*, and *The Shadows of Owls*

"Traditionally conceived, a poet is not only a maker but a prophet, a vates or
shaman. Prophecies are traditionally riddling and ambiguous, subject to tragic
misinterpretation. But the prescient lyrics of *Hawk on Wire* have an urgent clarity,
which reminds us that ecopoetry, whatever else it is, must include ecoprophecy.
Shifting from the lyric present into the cataclysmic future, or dreaming back
from post-apocalyptic end-times, Starbuck divines the consequences of climate
change in no uncertain terms. Yet more than foretelling, this fisherman poet
listens: to the ghosts of elders and outcasts (Mother Teresa, Mark Twain,
Galileo, the homeless), to fellow creatures (trout, lizard, otter, hawk) and to the
elements (earth, river, wind). Ecologists read the signs of unsustainability, poets
give them voice, none more compellingly than Starbuck. The question remains,
can we look up from our screens long enough to listen?"
—John Shoptaw, author of *Times Beach*

"This is truly a place-based book (Chewaucan River, Oregon) that focuses
on the larger story of climate change, and with the voice of a storyteller
whose message and imagery transcends the obvious with some poems
reading like parables. After all is said and done this is a must-read Eco-
classic with an important message for our time."
—Thomas Rain Crowe, author of *Zoro's Field: My Life in the Appalachian
Woods*

"His poems are informative, imaginative, and wise."
—Michael Spring, author of *Unfolding the Field*

"In the face of greed, willful ignorance, and 'alternative facts,' Starbuck's activist poetry is needed more than ever."
—Eric Magrane, coeditor of *The Sonoran Desert: A Literary Field Guide*

"For the reality of nature, we must go to poets like Starbuck who base their passions on what the scientists tell them. I recommend this book as a way of finding solace in sharing warning, wonder and joy."
—Daniela Gioseffi, American Book Award winning author, Editor: www.Eco-Poetry.org

"*Hawk on Wire* by Scott T. Starbuck is an essential collection of poetry. The poems in this collection ask the reader to dig deeper into her/his existence in connection with the natural world and each other."
—Teresa Mei Chuc, author of the poetry collections *Red Thread* and *Keeper of the Winds*

"Scott Starbuck's ecopoems are light-filled gems of the human spirit, wrought half from tears of delight, half from sorrow."
—Prartho Sereno, prize-winning author of *Elephant Raga* and *Call From Paris*

"Scott's poems are crisp, visual, sharp, no wasted words."
–Gail Entrekin, Editor, *Canary* (canarylitmag.org)

"Interspersed with salmon fishing and Starbuck's ghosts – Mother Teresa, Galileo, Twain and many others – *Hawk on Wire* deftly challenges and invites its readers to respond to anthropogenic climate change."
—Anne Elvey, Managing Editor, *Plumwood Mountain: An Australian Journal of Ecopoetry and Ecopoetics*

"Scott T. Starbuck's *Hawk on Wire* offers the hard truth on climate change and forces the question of whether art has the responsibility for advocating political positions. It does, and these poems do advocate — pointedly, crisply, and with no doubt as to our role and responsibility in catastrophic environmental change."
—Simmons B. Buntin, author of *Bloom, Riverfall,* and *Unsprawl,* and editor-in-chief of Terrain.org

Carbonfish Blues

Ecopoems
Scott T. Starbuck

Art
Guy Denning

Fomite
Burlington, VT

ISBN-978-1-944388-53-9
Library of Congress Control Number: 2018955203

Fomite
58 Peru Street
Burlington, VT 05401
www.fomitepress.com

"Fish will school in classrooms. Oysters will grow on submerged light poles."

— Jeff Goodell, *Rolling Stone* contributing editor, and author of *The Water Will Come: Rising Seas, Sinking Cities, and the Remaking of the Civilized World*

"I've spoken to prestigious scientists both on and off the record who believe that sooner rather than later, global population will be reduced to around 1 billion humans."

— Dahr Jamail, "Sixth Mass Extinction Ushers In Record-Breaking Wildfires and Heat," truthout.org, August 20, 2018, and author of *The End of Ice,* forthcoming from The New Press

Contents

One Sequoia to Another

This time
looks different.

Breadfruit

My South Pacific student said
when his people were hungry
they climbed trees for breadfruit
or went to bay to fish.

They slept when tired,
had time for family, friends, song.

"Life was better," he said. "Easier.
Not like here in Pacific Beach
where you work all day behind a counter
and don't make enough to live."

I think of him while peeling bluefin scales
off my arms --
eat, mate, avoid predators,
three ways to give thanks
to the Source of all.

Requiem 2 (for the now forgotten)

Sea Change

What if, glacially-speaking,
all Earth maps are wrong?

Walking among fireflies
and shining dead stars
what else will you question?

Wealth is Sea, Sky, and Community

The ability to find and harvest,
laugh and sing,
touch
and be touched,

greet in birth,
grieve in death –
petroglyph dancers
around ancient bonfires.

Big Oil vs Poetry

The night before the stone in his forehead,
Goliath had a terrible dream.

Laugh Out Loud Café

is so quiet it makes history museum
seem like carnival ride.

"What's up with the name?" I ask.
"Previous owner," I'm told,

and think of bad storms
that change coastlines,

Titanic lifeboats
leaving half full.

Bootprint

in curved-woman shape
with fake ripple tread
removing flesh from Earth,

beginning separation,
arrogance, deaf to what is
spoken from core

of ourselves
and everything real.

No Rescue

Hollywood shows another rescue but this is the story of men,
women, children who weren't rescued.

UN agencies noted over 8,500 migrants
drowned in Mediterranean

between 1 September 2015 and
September 2016 and number continues to grow.

Child-survivors across Europe
sell their bodies for cash and clothes.

United Nations High Commissioner for Refugees
notes there have never been

this many displaced people,
including after Second World War.

Beyond walls of flat screen TVs
in developed nations,

people pawn anything
to survive another night.

Alignment

With organic carrot cupcakes
and Dry-Erase pens
my friends battle BP, Exxon,
Chevron, Shell.

We bet energy
that governs all things
has life, purpose, direction,
and oil companies bet it doesn't.

What I like about my friends is
even if there were no God,
we would show up
to do the work
that must be done.

Remembering Celilo Falls

Some say nearby *She Who Watches* pictograph
is about looking over her children.
Others say it is a death mask about diseases
brought by settlers.

Maybe it will take tearing down upriver dams
to get young people to stop killing themselves.

One Raven

on hidden trail in Sitka spruce
looking for mate and food
before humans existed today
and after humans were gone.

Nel mezzo del cammin di nostra vita mi ritrovai per una selva oscura

All Arrows Out Point Inside

Bark beetles feast on our ignorance
until evergreens turn red as maples
on White House lawn.

Universal Zebra

Each time I think
I have Universe figured out,
it shows me I don't

so maybe the task
is acceptance
instead of steely wanting

what can not be known,
freed and trapped
as we are in human flesh.

On side of a hippie van:
It's not about going anywhere,
It's about being.

Climate Reality

"I will not beg the world leaders to care for our future. I will instead let them know change is coming whether they like it or not."
—15-year-old Greta Thunberg, "descendant[ ] of Svante Arrhenius, the Nobel-prize-winning scientist who in 1896 first calculated the greenhouse effect caused by carbon dioxide emissions," to "conference of nearly 200 nations" at 2018 UN climate change summit as reported by Damian Carrington in The Guardian article "'Our leaders are like children,' school strike founder tells climate summit," December 4, 2018

Your parents said
if you followed rules
you would be okay.

Grade school, middle school,
high school, college,
made same promise.

Your employer went
one step further
to better than okay.

The truth is,
as you discovered,
they lied.

Warrior's Story of Whale Bankers

Imagine some whales decide
they want to own the sea
and other whales
must devote lifetimes
to bringing them shrimp and krill.

"Whatever you believe
about your ocean birthright
is wrong," they say,
hiring narwhals
to harpoon in gut
anyone who disagrees.

Young whales in pens
are taught to be still
and quiet followers.

Whale bankers invent Whale Gods
bestowing Divine Right of Whales
until, eventually, most whales believe
ordinary whales
were never intended
to swim free in moonlit surface,
listen to or sing
ancient whale songs.

Warrior Says One Tree's Greatest Blessing

deep in woods
of distant valley
was to spend her life
free from eyes
or interest
of any man.

Once Upon a Time

there were salmon in river,
elk in forest,
owls in old barns,
song in heart.

For leaders, however,
and those before,
oil was more sacred
than Jesus.

Bear Shadow

I go to river to catch fish.

I speak to humans to learn truth.

If there are no fish in river,
I lose interest.

If there is no truth in human,
I lose interest.

Years go by.
Rivers, humans, galaxies fade.

Natural laws and soul laws ensure
nothing changes but faces.

Rosetta Poem

"New DNA studies suggest that all humans descended from
a single African ancestor who lived some 60,000 years ago."
— Hillary Mayell, "Geneticist Searches for DNA of 'Adam,'
the First Human," news.nationalgeographic.com, June 24, 2005

If plants and animals
have a common ancestor
(they do)

and nearly all 7.6 billion humans
have same ancient grandfather
(they do)

is it possible distorted language
has been real enemy
all along?,

that blue/green poets
are needed now
more than ever?

What is the sacred song
of each pound dog
before injection,

Pacific island
before saltwater inundation?

Titanic Radio

By now you know,
or will soon,
our great unsinkable ship
is sinking
and we don't have
enough lifeboats
for everyone.

Our ship's owner
saved money
       installing partial
bulkheads
allowing water to spill
over the top.

It's live and learn
or, for those in 2nd and 3rd class,
maybe not.

Carbonfish Blues

Some on *Titanic*,
like Esther Hart, felt what was
more real than what could be seen,
smelled, heard, tasted, touched,
until cold saltwater baptized
everyone.

She stayed up each night
fully dressed,
waiting for impact,
and when it came,
she was ready in a way
none can be for abrupt climate change.

The refuge this time
is going inward,
making peace with yourself
and those you love.

The disasters of war 11

Depoe Bay Poem

Dad, a Korean War vet, recalled a shell was stuck in launcher
so officer glanced in barrel which took his head clean off.
"Too much college, and not enough life" I heard,
18 and leaving for sea in pea soup offshore fog.

Soon

salmon cans will be opened like rubies.

Oranges will be rare as diamonds.

People will recall shopping at Safeway.

When Coral Reefs Vanished

Reef-Co, a Tokyo animation firm,
invented an artificial reef
with artificial fish, neon corals,
artificial pelicans in artificial sky,
artificial boats, artificial sharks,
laser manta rays, sea turtles,
shipwrecks and artificial people
lit by carbon-burning electricity
that killed them all.

Remembering Bob

Spaceship passing buildings on mostly dead planet:

"They should have tried solar."

"Or cellular, as in biology instead of technology."

"Or looked past ends of their wallets
while they had time."

"At least they produced Bob Marley.
That was something."

"Yes," everyone agrees. "That was something."

Floating Plastic Jesus

"One million seabirds and 100,000 marine mammals die globally each year due to ingestion of or entanglement in plastics."
—RISE ABOVE PLASTICS, O'ahu Chapter of Surfrider Foundation

Some spirituality is injection molded and mass produced,
arms raised over albatross in beer loops,
belly-up dolphin in ghost net
in Pacific Garbage Patch
widely reported as "three times the size of France."

The real Jesus is known to have said "Forgive them
for they don't know what they're doing."

Warrior's Story of The Last Wild Otter Near Otter Crest, Oregon, 1906

"The last known native Oregon sea otter is thought to have been killed near Newport in 1906. Its pelt later sold for $900. "
—Michael Milstein in *Oregon Live*, March 14, 2001

The autumn moon
says it's time to mate
but no amount of splashing
or singing
will bring her home
once she has gone
to that other world.

Thousands of generations
cracking open clams
with a rock on chest,
playing in surf,
and teaching pups
secret caverns
beneath the swell

have come to
a rich lady in New York
wearing skin
of your lover
and you, between your cries,
listening to sound of gulls
and crashing waves
in Pacific darkness.

Even If

nuclear bombs are disarmed,
war mellows to peace,
climate breakdown is solved,
ozone layer healed,
oceans are restored,
our sun will one day oscillate,
scorching everything to ash.

The point is
don't squander the gift.

Listen closely
alone
on an evening beach
for what you are
to do.

The hand of man (dispossessed)

Invader

"Total number of deaths attributed to conflict diamond mining[:] 3 Million"
—statisticbrain.com/conflict-diamond-statistics

Rhinos for horns

Elephants for tusks

Salmon for dams

Coral reefs for coal

Diamonds for death

Mountains for deserts

Future for zeros and ones

Future for zeros and ones

Future for zeros and ones

Future for zeros and ones

Future for zeros and ones

Future for zeros and ones

News Fragments

"When we try to pick out anything by itself,
we find it hitched to everything else in the universe."
—John Muir

A fake bus stop to nowhere calms Alzheimer's patients
outside Benrath Senior Center in Düsseldorf, Germany.

[Fake] — In Hawai'i, parents and children expecting nuclear war
hid in bathtubs until notified it was false alarm.

[Death] — 75,000 years ago, when Mt. Toba erupted,
the entire human population dropped to less than 10,000.

[Loss] — *Los Angeles Times* reporter Robert Lee Hotz noted "NASA lost
its $125-million Mars Climate Orbiter because spacecraft engineers failed

to convert from English to metric measurements when exchanging
vital data before the craft was launched."

[Error] — In 2017 scientists taught an orca in France to speak English
but couldn't teach humans to speak orca, peace, or life.

$450

is the price, according to Dr. Veerabhadran Ramanathan,
"per person per year in the top one billion people" to save over
3 billion people that may otherwise die from exposure
to 130 degree plus heat
35 years from now if humans fail to convert energy sources
from coal and fossil fuels
to "solar, wind, hydro, and possibly nuclear."

$450 is less than half the price of new iPhone X,
or about one fifth the cost of Superbowl Ticket,
or one 13.3333333 billionth projected cost of Iraq War counting interest.
Imagine one eight pound girl baking because it was more important

for you to surf Internet, be there for kickoff, silence yourself on war.
You, by the numbers, Mr. and Mrs. Average North American,
will consume 1,820 chickens, 70 turkeys, 7 cows, 35 hogs,

will watch 127, 750 hours of TV, burn 35,000 gallons of gas,
spend 114,975 hours on computer,

and what, for all you have taken, being 5% world population
producing half the world's garbage, using 24% of her energy,
and being the largest carbon-emitting nation in history,
will you give back
to this blue gem you call home?*

* Statistics found using google.com

A Million Underwater Vehicles in Texas

"The storm may have ruined up to one million vehicles along the Texas Gulf Coast,
according to automotive data firm Black Book."
— "Harvey may have wrecked up to 1M cars and trucks" by Nathan Bomey and Aamer
Madhani, *USA TODAY*, Aug. 31, 2017

are going to make buyers unhappy
when they realize someone else's problem
is suddenly theirs,

not much different
than some North Americans
completely ignoring climate breakdown.

Milkweed

"Monarchs need these plants," Kate shows, "or they die
on flights from Nova Scotia to Mexico."

I think of baby monkeys suffering from lack of touch
on wire mothers, others horror-stricken in Harlow's

isolation chambers up to two years, still more
under researchers' welding masks for men to study

face recognition in preferred way
to see what's real and meaningful

as we share 96 percent of DNA
and hidden maze of neural networks.

All around us similarly insane men
destroy Earth and everything on it.

But it is still wonderful to watch monarchs
like soulful strangers

traveling so close from so far away.

We who know it as broken business

What There Is, and What We See

In the beginning
was bird
and bird had no wings
because it didn't need them.

It swam like a fish
in uterus
of Universe,

but even that
was not the first
because it's origin

was invisible birds
from long before song
when everything was

one song of
clear white light
containing rainbow colors
of all birds.

If you want to know birds,
you must know this.

Unspoken

To some, name of Creator is unspoken
like name of Western red cedar cathedral
or initiation cave on secret path,
mountain ledge, or ancient salmon graveyard/birthyard.

Deep silences and emerald currents speak
what must be said.
It's about respect for what's alive
in ways it takes listeners, and not name-makers,

to understand.

Climate Poem Written
Before We Lose Arctic Ice

"If we lose the Arctic, we lose the globe."
—President Niinistö of Finland in Joint Press Conference
with President Trump, August 28, 2017 cited
at www.whitehouse.gov/briefings-statements

In Andes storm
if you were on plane
you knew would crash

would you sing,
laugh, cry, pray,
speak with man beside you,

write letter
to those you loved
or should have?

Would you listen
to God
that made you?

When Heat Killed Internet

people looked up, met, and talked.
It was painful, at first, then
they saw ravens, fir, mountains
like babies seeing sunlight
first time.

Dying Soldier

cries
then laughs

as spirit departs
uniform

in recognition
of life defending

a castle
that doesn't exist

in this new
more-real land,

and what's worse,
never existed.

Gaza hospital

The Builders' Sons Discuss History and Literature

I dream I'm in a posh London hotel where I work as janitor
while builders' sons are down to serious business
planning fate of world.

To them, the G20 Summit in Pittsburgh, IMF, World Bank,
US Congress, UN, and Fed are jokes.

I sit under table, drink lemonade, and listen to them talk
about growing need for population control and
challenges from new builders' sons in Russia, India, and China.

"Hell, 'Drunkards of Menkaure' enjoyed building the pyramid.
Their hieratic scripts reveal they made a game out of it" says a Luxembourgian.
"Shakespeare understood power is always about human psychology."

"If that doesn't work, we threaten economic war
to motivate the uncooperative," says an Englishman.
"If they try to change reserve currency too soon,
we bomb hell out of them, figuratively speaking."

An American says "We start by convincing them the same way
Tom Sawyer tricked kids into painting that fence.
If that doesn't work, I agree with the Englishman."

I can tell by their conversation they are educated, and
most believe they serve humanity by ruling humanity.

"Pay no attention to that man behind the curtain," said the Wizard of Oz,
written by L. Frank Baum, whose father, Benjamin, many sources note,
"made a fortune in Pennsylvania oil."

Rosebud

Citizen Kane
learned
the hard way

what matters
in end
and what doesn't.

A lie
only has to be
kept up

until
believer
is dead,

or planet.

Arctic Nightmare

"The Average American Melts 645 Square Feet of Arctic Ice Every Year." —Robinson Meyer, November 3, 2016, theatlantic.com/science

"Geoengineering Is Not a Solution to Climate Change" [. . . .] "[E]very scientist, including the council authors, is convinced that if albedo modification is implemented and not followed by a program of global emission reductions, then we are almost certainly finished."
—Clive Hamilton, March 10, 2015, *Scientific American*

I'm sorry to say Blue Ocean Event,
or mostly ice-free Arctic,
has been predicted by 2040
and scientists keep moving up the date.

Ten years after it happens,
we may have an ice-free Arctic year round
followed by melting Greenland
that will raise seas 20 feet

triggering panic and migration
from coastal cities
where hundreds of millions live.

The party of industry, even here,
will be over.

I Don't Want to Rock the Boat of Industrial Civilization. I Want to Capsize It

nonviolently,

with a focus on sustainability.

Each new car must post
"Square Feet of Arctic Ice Cost Per Year."

Same goes for refrigerators,
air conditioners, heaters,
politicians.

Each airplane flight,
pound of red meat,
hour of TV
and cell phone.

After Species Bottleneck

if you're lucky
you may be reincarnated beside undersea heat vent
as bacteria or archaea,
then, in few million years, as relatively glorious
giant tube worm, clam, limpet or shrimp.

Forget rock music, surfing, snowboarding,
undressing beautiful lover,
walking your dog and child
through tidepools
near used-to-be green canopy of forest.

You will unlearn human distraction from soul.

Warrior is a River Watcher

Sometimes if you watch
long enough
a rock grows fins.

Other times a branch
becomes deer antler

or oak hole
face of owl.

Once, when I was nine
in evening woods
my fear of dark changed
to fear of going home.

Poem on Redwood

Most days I would rather meet
tree than person.

Tree has real roots and heartwood.
It feels water, cloud shapes, sun.

Some giants in Jedediah Smith State Park
have seen over 14,000 full moons

compared to men who act
like they haven't seen any.

As Climate *Titanic* Sinks

"The Icelandic Families Tracking Climate Change With Measuring Tape."
—Gloria Dickie and *Undark*, theatlantic.com, June 6, 2018

Men fight over
whether it is sinking,
though a tape measure
from deck to waterline
makes it clear enough.

Until after the dust of a million suns

Not My Tribe

destroyed huge salmon runs with unfishladdered 500-foot Grand Coulee Dam in 1939,
released radioactive iodine-131 in "Green Run" over 200 miles from Hanford in 1949,
made Oregon a "whites-only" state, banning nonwhites under exclusion laws until 1959,
delisted Samish Indian Nation, a signatory to the Point Elliot Treaty of 1855, in 1969,
released radioactive gases and radioactive iodine at Three Mile Island Station in 1979,
spilled 10.8 million gallons of oil from Exxon Valdez to Prince William Sound in 1989,
named Snake River the USA's most endangered from dam-caused salmon loss in 1999,
failed to prevent BP Oil Spill by avoiding acoustic-triggered shutoff valves in 2009,
melted early 200,000 square miles of Bearing Sea ice from climate change before 2019,
threatened, by carbon and methane releases, billions of humans and nonhumans by 2029,
killed, by avoidable carbon and methane releases, billions of humans and nonhumans by 2039.

Distraction Machine

works harder than ever, reporting
mushroom hunter finding two headed deer,

omitting Bering sea ice melting 30 days early
risking global food security from heat.

So this is what it means as Oz's curtain rises,
and last COSTCO trucks arrive in frenzy.

In spring 1849 Louisburgh Irish Starvation
rich let poor starve in front yards.

Do you think it will be different now?
How will humanity retain humanity

as oceans die, and neighbor turns against neighbor?
Do barracuda have mercy on anchovies?

When lesser churches of business and industry fade,
bicycles outcompete cars unable to get gas,

will Oregon withhold water from
Californians starved by drought? Yes.

Will Washington shut out Oregonians
as Oregon is overrun? Yes.

Will Canada and Alaska follow suit? Yes and yes.
Will desperate N. Americans with guns use them? Yes.

On a three day media fast, I reflect

I have more pity on the distracted and ignorant
than Nature will.

Vercingetorix Knew in 52 B. C.

the only way to defeat Rome
was to burn stored grain
in village of Avaricum

stretching food supply lines
and forcing Roman retreat.
Elders there voted "No."

and after siege of 27 days
Caesar killed 39,200
including women and children.

Sometimes, as with climate
change, sacrifice is painful
but "No." means nearly
everyone dies.

$10,000 Apple

An apple treeless world
will be hard for humans
but worse on birds.

Preachers will have to
change fruit of knowledge
of good and evil.

First Bird to Fly on Earth

didn't get there overnight, but
started with small hops.

Helene, who waters garden,
says if you take care of plants

they watch over your dreams.

Welcome to the Future

According to stories of Pacific Northwest Coast natives,
raven brought light into universe.

In 2017 Orange County Water District gave
human urine recycled as free bottled water.

Near Santa Barbara, the former Ocean Meadows Golf Course
became The North Campus Open Space (NCOS) Restoration Project.

Still, in 2018 carbon and methane emissions grew, Earth heated,
and Arctic bowhead, narwhal, and beluga are in increasing danger

as Arizona's wild horses die of drought, and
sooner or later we must individually decide

if we will take the suicide pill of apathy with others.
The brown eye of a raven up close

is enough to convince anyone otherwise.

Rain

Years ago I found a book
in a Warrenton, Oregon charter office,
Everything I Learned
in 50 Years of Fishing

and when I opened it
all pages were blank.
I laughed at its humility
but my 10 years at sea

showed its hard-won wisdom:
Always be mindful
and ready for anything.

Recycle

politicians
into nameless moonfish
inside their mothers,

teachers
into students
of students,

businessmen
into birds
saving skies

flying places
thought
impossible..

L'ari sadi carnot iii

Ancient Forest

People stare at iPhones
but what about listening

to voice of sea,
geese migrations,

salmon splashes,
cedar arms in wind,

like ages before
when men and women knew

quench soul hunger
first thing in morning

before saying anything
to anyone.

The Fear Fly

The fear fly returns
from a childhood dream hissing --
"You will never breathe deep
as you did before the loss."

"You will always be alone.
Love is a divine lie.
Climate change or cancer will kill
everyone you know."

A walk among driftwood fires
brings an older, wiser sea voice
saying *the Fear Fly is afraid
and comes to us*

*as a test of what is real
between shoulders, ears,
people and
shooting stars.*

Union Pacific Rolls by Troutdale on Schedule

with its mustard engines,
corpses of Douglas fir,
oil cars like those derailed
in Moser June 3, 2016
when a woman lost her shepherd
in the explosion,
and most everyone lost faith,
if they ever had it,
in slick promises, glossy photos.

Columbia River Prophecy

Climate change makes old river
a cioppino of salmon, shad,
14 foot long sturgeon
eaten by oil monster
in men's hearts.

Future children will look
at historic photos and ask
"What were you thinking?"

In Slow Motion

You, on sidelines
of climate fight,
are no better
than a distracted mother
who baked her kids
in hot car.

The Hunger

You led me to a night hawk
circling orchards for mice,

lantern moon,

diamond eyes
of an 80-year-old sturgeon
cruising river bank
like a forgotten Indian god.

We walked in the hour
skeleton oaks
reached out of hiding
to touch,

just a short time
before human tide moved in
and this place became
invisible.

Your opinion is worthless

Mushroom Hunting on Black Friday

Crowds of red spawning chinook
and lounging elk
celebrate day

of autumn abundance,
oak leaf colors,
along hidden river.

Once, out of habit
I watched a mossy TV
dumped below cliff.

Far from electricity,
it was home for sow bugs
and centipedes.

It was there I saw my eyes
in silent core
watched by clouds and sky.

Memory

Once, during 7th grade football practice
my team helped corner runaway horses.
Nostrils flared, eyes shot lightning,
but there were five of them and forty of us
yelling, stomping, trapping
until owner arrived with trailer.

That night I dreamed thousands of years back
when St. Anthony's school was a stand of red cedar
and church a meadow.
Horses were friends.
We learned about healing herbs,
dances of masking and unmasking.

Father's Day,

pitchfork that fell
off truck,

dead deer on side
of Highway 84,

rust-colored clouds,

broken machinery
by shed,

so much irrigation
wasted to wind.

Flood Year

rivers took back streets
and patterns of our lives
were set by clouds.

Old people remembered
Tony's Fish Market
selling from rowboat

and neighbors sandbagging
each other's homes.
Salmon crossed highways,

easy picking
for pitchfork
or kids on hands and knees.

Poem for Abraham

Instead of cell phone
he carries a shell
for when he must hear
sound of waves

or commune with higher
ancient self
that crawled out
of nearby sea.

Oregon Forest Reckoning

Here you can make peace
with Eternal Invisible Flame
of water beings, sky beings,
earth beings, fire beings,
gray mist days
rolling in
through Sitka spruce.

Watching, just watching

Anchor House

If you want to be rooted in place
stay with ancient hungers --
wild berries, flute, worship,
marriage, sex, listening to wind in firs,
river song, migrating geese.

Stranger

"In a 100 years wild salmon runs south of Canada will be reduced to remnant runs."
—Bob Lackey, Professor of Fisheries at Oregon State University

Future children will hear story of when
stranger wandered into town armed with harp,
got food, lodging, women, disappeared
and became legend.

 "Years passed, and someone found a blood-stained
knife under moss beside harp, strings gone
but ghost music still playing in alders and firs."

The truth will become
the stranger, which was salmon,
changed into man, river a harp,
when real story of losing salmon and orcas
grew too sad to tell.

The Scar and the Spell

The lack of ability for people to be fully themselves
made all past, present, and future wars necessary.
This is why we sit, meditate, pray.

A child raised by wolves is loyal to the pack.
A child raised by sky is loyal to sky.

Local Knowledge

And one year the Patriarch said
"Let's stop going to sea,
and sell fish instead."

"Let someone else's son
lose a father."

"Let someone else's wife
lose a husband.

"Let someone else's brother
lose a brother."

As years went by
away from spirit helpers,

once fearless sons and grandsons
became worthless doctors,
evil bankers, vacant lawyers,
corrupt politicians.

Stepford Congress

Smiles,
glazed eyes,
robotic,

obedient,
attractive,
bought

by oil companies,
and dying
with them.

Heliocentric

Maybe the last living tree on Earth
sends a signal the experiment is done,

and Energy that governs all decides,
impartial as gravity,

who among zebras and nonzebras
gets recycled, and who is left

as hoofprint in the wind.

Observer Post 9

Let us say Earth is studied by a distant class
where the professor notes "Each week
they drive to 'poison stations'
with many other options
as CO_2 and methane skyrocket."

Governments, militaries, citizens
express a twisted death wish.
"Convenience?" asks a student.
"Insanity?" asks another.
"Yes and yes" says the professor

calculating years to human extinction.
"But there they call it 'politics.'"

Oceans Away

people are affected by what you do, think, feel, believe.

You toss your computer, and Chinese people get sick
from lead and mercury.

You think climate change is a hoax, and Marshall Islands sink.

You feel entitled because of your hard work,
and people everywhere starve.

You believe this poem doesn't matter,
and are reincarnated as a cockroach.

What They Don't Teach in Most U. S. Schools

Nuclear war in 1945 meant
we die or survive together.

Here at the End, I Remember

kid bored out of his mind
changing commas into hawks
and quadratic equations
into dolphins.

Once, he received detention
for attaching doughy cinnamon
elephant ears
to garden saints.

That day, even the old priest
laughed
before scolding him.

What was more important?

Grammar?

Math?

Another solemn garden?

A Prayer Under New Moon

May dry winds sweep away
each track
and darkness echo
cry of wolves,

night sky flower anew
for those who arrive.

Paradis est ici 21

Acknowledgments

Grateful acknowledgment is made to the following publications in which these poems first appeared, or are forthcoming.

2018 Word and Image Anthology: Hoffman Center for the Arts: "The Fear Fly" and "Floating Plastic Jesus"

The Analog Sea Review: "Ancient Forest"

Autumn Sky Poetry: "Warrior's Story of The Last Wild Otter Near Otter Crest, Oregon, 1906" (published under the title "The Last Wild Otter Near Otter Crest, Oregon, 1906")

Blueline (at SUNY Potsdam): "Here at the End, I Remember"

Blotterature: "Sea Change"

Hawai'i Review: "Dying Soldier"

Cascadia Review: "Father's Day"

For Love of Orcas (anthology published by Wandering Aengus Press): "Stranger"

Owen Wister Review: "Warrior is a River Watcher" (published under the title "River Watcher")

The Raven Chronicles: "Laugh Out Loud Café," and "Warrior Comes From the Land of Scalded Souls" (published under the title "What I Think of American History")

Rune (at Massachusetts Institute of Technology): "The Builders' Sons Discuss History and Literature"

Scott T. Starbuck's Trees, Fish, and Dreams (blog): "Big Oil vs Poetry," "Remembering Celilo Falls" (YouTube film / poem)

Wildflower: "A Prayer Under New Moon"

Windfall: "Warrior's Story of The Last Wild Otter Near Otter Crest, Oregon, 1906" (published under the title "The Last Wild Otter Near Otter Crest, Oregon, 1906")

"Here at the End, I Remember" appeared in the chapbook *The Other History* . . . by FutureCycle Press.

"Warrior is a River Watcher," "Warrior Says One Tree's Greatest Blessing," "Warrior's Story of The Last Wild Otter Near Otter Crest, Oregon, 1906," and "Warrior's Story of Whale Bankers" appeared in the chapbook *The Warrior Poems* by Pudding House Publications.

About the Author

Scott T. Starbuck's *Hawk on Wire: Ecopoems* (Fomite, 2017) was selected from over 1,500 entries as a Montaigne Medal Finalist at Eric Hoffer Awards for "the most thought-provoking books." Written at a PLAYA climate change residency, it was a July 2017 "Editor's Pick" at Newpages.com along with *The Collected Stories of Ray Bradbury*, and featured at Yale Climate Connections. There is a 24-minute YouTube of his book launch sponsored by La Jolla Historical Society's WEATHER ON STEROIDS EXHIBIT. In addition to being a poet, Starbuck participated in, and presented at, the UCSD Climate Curriculum Workshop, gathering ideas for his science-based poems. His climate ecoblog is *Trees, Fish, and Dreams* with over 42,000 pageviews from across the globe, and his "Manifesto from Poet on a Dying Planet" is online at *Split Rock Review*. He was a core speaker at the 17th annual California Higher Education Sustainability Conference (CHESC) hosted in 2018 by University of California, Santa Barbara.

About the Artist

Guy Denning is a contemporary artist, born in the UK and now living and working in France. More work can be seen at www.guydenning.org

Photo © Ti Adam

Fomite

About Fomite

A fomite is a medium capable of transmitting infectious organisms from one individual to another.

"The activity of art is based on the capacity of people to be infected by the feelings of others." Tolstoy, *What Is Art?*

Writing a review on Amazon, Good Reads, Shelfari, Library Thing or other social media sites for readers will help the progress of independent publishing. To submit a review, go to the book page on any of the sites and follow the links for reviews. Books from independent presses rely on reader to reader communications.

For more information or to order any of our books, visit
http://www.fomitepress.com/FOMITE/Our_Books.html

More Titles from Fomite...

Novels

Fomite

Fomite

Fomite

Stories

Fomite

Made in the USA
San Bernardino, CA
21 December 2018